The Edge of Being

by the same author

*

POEMS

TRIAL OF A JUDGE

THE STILL CENTRE

RUINS AND VISIONS

SELECTED POEMS

POEMS OF DEDICATION

THE
EDGE OF BEING

by

STEPHEN
SPENDER

FABER AND FABER
24 Russell Square
London

First published in mcmxlix
by Faber and Faber Limited
24 Russell Square London W.C.1
Printed in Great Britain by
R. MacLehose and Company Limited
The University Press Glasgow

To
NATASHA

Contents

9

O Omega, Invocation

O, thou O, opening O,
Passing from earth into a sky
Drained of last wings,
Then beyond the empyrean blue
Passing passing through light
Into space too white for seeing—

O, thou O, passing beyond
Light, into sound,
Where one trumpet sustains
Concentrated symphonies
On the peak of one note,
Then passing passing beyond
To all sound silence—

O, thou O, beyond silence
Invoking gods and goddesses,
The owl-eyed, the up-finger-pointing,
Imaged flesh changing
From idea into form
Then back to bodilessness,
Continual metamorphosis
Of gods changing to godlessness—

O, thou O, returning to
Thyself, O, whose black
Hoop, circling on white
Paper, vanishes where the eye
Springs through thee, O,
Beyond space silence image,
O thou, word of beginning
Oh with what wordless end.

O Night O Trembling Night

O night O trembling night O night of sighs
O night when my body was a rod O night
When my mouth was a vague animal cry
Pasturing on her flesh   O night
When the close darkness was a nest
Made of her hair and filled with my eyes

(O stars impenetrable above
Each fragile life here where it lies
Among the petals falling fields of time
O night revolving all our dark away)

O day O gradual day O sheeted light
Covering her body as with dews
Until I brushed her sealing sleep away
To read once more in the uncurtained day
Her naked love, my great good news.

On the Third Day

(To W. H. A.)

On the first summer day I lay in the valley.
Above rocks the sky sealed my eyes with a leaf.
The grass licked my skin. The flowers bounds my nostrils
With scented cotton threads. The soil invited
My hands and feet to press down and grow roots.
Bees and grasshoppers drummed over
Crepitations of thirst rising from dry stones,
And the ants rearranged my ceaseless thoughts
Into different patterns for ever the same.
Then the blue wind fell out of the air
And the sun beat down till I became of wood
Glistening brown beginning to warp.

On the second summer day I climbed through the forest
(Huge tent anchored to the mountainside by roots)
My direction was defeated by weight of numbers
I could not see the wood for the trees.
The darkness lay under the leaves, in a war
Against light, which occasionally penetrated
Splintering spears through several interstices
And dropping bright clanging shields on the soil.
Silence was stitched through with thinnest pine needles
And bird songs were stifled behind a hot hedge.
My feet became as heavy as logs.
I drank up all the air of the forest.
My mind changed to amber enclosing dead flies.

On the third summer day I sprang from the forest
Into the wonder of a white snow-tide.
Alone with the sun's wild whispering wheel

Grinding sparks of secret light on frozen fields,
Every burden fell from me, I threw the forest from my back,
The valley dwindled to a human world departed,
Torn to shreds by clouds of the sun's shifting visions.
Above the snowfield, one rock against the sky
Shaped from utter silence a black naked tune,
A violin when the tune forgets the instrument
And the use of the ear is only as gate
To receive into the mind the sound's soundless form.

Awaking

Ever the same, forever new!
The gravel path searching the Way;
The cobwebs beaded with the dew;
The empty waiting of new day.

So I remember each new morning
From childhood, when pebbles amaze.
Outside my window, the forewarning
Glitter of those days.

The sense felt behind darkened walls,
An amber-solid world, a lake
Of light, through which light falls.
It is this to which I wake.

Then the sun shifts the trees around
And overtops the sky, and throws
House, horse and rider to the ground
With knockout shadows.

The whole sky opens to an O,
The cobweb dries, the petals spread,
The clocks grow beards, the people go
Walking over their graves, the dead.

The world's a circle where all moves
Before after after before.
Such joy my new-awaking proves
Each day—until I start to care.

(1930-1948)

15

Faust's Song

Oh, that I might be one with that moonlight
Which spreads its tiger stare across these books,
Through the high barred pane where, night after night,
My endless longing meets her endless looks!

Freed from these cobwebs, dust and phials of knowledge,
Would I might in her hell of heaven flit:
Be stripped in dews and rolled through grass and hedge
And sigh in caverns of her sensual spirit.

To wake on peaks at dawn among the inhuman
Rose-towering dreams—O peacocks, fountains, sighs—
Reborn in the blonde landscape of a woman,
And dying in the river of her eyes!

Judas Iscariot

The eyes of twenty centuries
Pursue me along corridors to where
I am painted at their ends on many walls.
  Ever-revolving futures recognize
This red hair and red beard, where I am seated
Within the dark cave of the feast of light.
  Out of my heart-shaped shadow I stretch my hand
Across the white table into the dish
But not to dip the bread. It is as though
The cloth on each side of one dove-bright face
Spread dazzling wings on which the apostles ride
Uplifting them into the vision
Where their eyes watch themselves enthroned.
    My russet hand across the dish
Plucks enviously against one feather
—But still the rushing wings spurn me below!

    Saint Sebastian of wickedness
I stand: all eyes legitimate arrows piercing through
The darkness of my wickedness. They recognize
My halo hammered from thirty silver pieces
And the hemp rope around my neck
Soft as that Spirit's hanging arms
When on my cheek he answered with the kiss
Which cuts for ever—
                My strange stigmata,
All love and hate, all fire and ice!

    But who betrayed whom? O you,
Whose light gaze forms the azure corridor
Though which those other pouring eyes

Arrow into me—answer! Who
Betrayed whom? Who had foreseen
All, from the first? Who read
In his mind's light from the first day
That the kingdom of heaven on earth must always
Reiterate the garden of Eden,
And each day's revolution be betrayed
Within man's heart, each day?

                      Who wrapped
The whispering serpent round the tree
And hung between the leaves the glittering purse
And trapped the fangs with God-appointed poison?
Who knew
I must betray the truth, and made the lie
Betray its truth in me?

     Those hypocrite eyes which aimed at you
Now aim at me. And yet, beyond their world
We are alone, eternal opposites,
Each turning on his pole of truth, your pole
Invisible light, and mine
Becoming what man is. We stare
Across two thousand years, and heaven, and hell,
Into each other's gaze.

Ice

(TO M. M. B.)

She came in from the snowing air
Where icicle-hung architecture
Strung white fleece round the baroque square.
I saw her face freeze in her fur
And my lips seemed to fetch quick fire
From the firelit corner of the room
Where I had waited in my chair.
I kissed this fire against her skin
And watched the warmth make her cheeks bloom
While at my care her smiling eyes
Shone with the health of the ice
Outside, whose brilliance they brought in.
That day, until this, I forgot.
How is it now I so remember,
Who, when she came indoors, saw not
The passion of her white December?

Returning to Vienna 1947

(TO W. J. S.)

I

Feminine Vienna, where the Ring's
Inner street embossed with palaces
Guarded the city virginal cathedral—

And in the central Graben Square
The swaggering column of a monument
Burst out of the past to commemorate
Some long-forgotten once-resisted rape
Whether by plague or Turk I now forget—

I saw the soot-stained marble battering-ram
Uplift its cloud of cherubim
Clustering on its cross like bees
Perpetually reborn virginities
Vienna ascendant against dissolving cloud—

Through summers of between-war dream
Vienna lay upon its plain
Each war one hand on the horizon's rim—

Summer already seemed hallucination
Of leaves painted upon a canvas screen
Behind which wicked forces laid
Their plot to end all summers—

Obscene kisses
Of first and second wars clucking
Behind the hedge of leaf-eyed lovers
Made boys' flesh conjuring their girls of rose

Their very lust sign of the time's decay
Their innocence sign of its impotence
By contrast with that breeding of steel furies—

Preparing a world's childless juvenescence.

II

Yet there the flower of my first flesh unfolded
Among her woods her cafés her stone draperies
There my youth was an eyed prow descrying
Beyond the storms of my crossed years
A fleshscape woven of fiery fleece—

Vienna of my loving my first woman
She and I had senses canopied
With luminous trilling leaves of beech
Knotted to boughs against transparent skies—

When I laid my head against her dress
Scented with flesh and porous with cicadas
Beyond the dark I saw the brooched lights shine
Within the earth I heard the deep warm pulse
Vienna's life was lying in my arms
While music shaping through me was the airs
Yearning through Vienna woods
To chisel sculpture of orchestras.

III

Beyond herself-myself   Beyond
Our interpenetrated human forest
Swallowing the absence in our meeting places
Beyond the vowing lipped abandonment
Of both to one meeting loneliness

Beyond the crystal bowl of our joined gaze—
There was reality, the flaw
Within the golden crystal bowl, where life
Was not entirely love nor even
Baroque frozen in dolphin attitudes
But was the unemployed who starved—

We saw their burning bodies like the spokes
Of cartwheels thrown down near dried ponds
We saw that prearranged disorder
Where socialist heroes who denied their souls
To hammer from their time-bound bodies
A world where workers would wear haloes
Each of his gain for what he gave—

Were shot at by the white-faced cynics
Who with their iron and stiff arms destroyed
These little optimists of tenements—

We saw the small empiric saints shot down
Shot down singing in their tenements
Their Karl Marx Hof and Goethe Haus
Killed by the realists of disenchantment.

IV

There where our love seemed hewn like crystal
Into a bowl where all times met
Within the stillness created by our looking—
Where the vision of the dead seemed absolute
Frozen within centennial architecture
Which futures rubbed like breezes over leaves
Lacing some lines and cherishing some gold—

22

The seeming permanence was an illusion
For what was real was transitory dust
True to our time dust blowing into dust
The dust a vital inward spring with power
To shatter history-frozen visions
And burst through cities and break down their walls—

The great stones of Vienna were but blocks
Lying across the present dissolution
Against that powerful decadence as weak
As senile oaths stuttering into dust—
And plunging deeper into our eyes' bowl
I saw there in our gaze what breaks the heart—

The tears and bloodshot vein of seeing
The outer world destroy the inner world.

V

Throughout that summer there was still some glory
Sunset lucidity which bathed
The Graben's cloud-insulting monument
And statues of extravagant angels
Wrestling in marble from the marble past
Perpetually reflowering virginal
Vienna against dissolving dust—

Gilded amid Baroque I mourned
The ruined shell of Karl Marx Hof and wept
The fallen workers amongst the ruined angels—

Their tears of pearl rolling down cheeks of gold
Changing to diamonds where they splashed the pavement—

23

And murdered Wallisch seemed a martyr
With raised right hand and marble frown
Moving in death through shell-torn tenements—

His hand with dying gesture signed
Such white and simple freedoms as could be
Chiselled on palaces for all humanity—

Where noble pasts with noble futures fuse.

VI

Vienna Vienna fallen in Vienna—

Within one instant of one night
One flash which made the streets one white—

Within one flash of time one knife
That held Vienna mirrored on its blade—

Then plunged—a hilt of diving wings—
To break the image into fragments—

The statued angel fell upon her knees
Agony shrouded with collapsing roofs

Her dereliction strewn before her history
Her marble feet broken—

                                  Then roared
The chariot of the smoking wide explosion
Dragging Vienna in tumbrils round her Ring—

Vienna Vienna fallen within Vienna.

VII

I come back to the fallen to the dust
The broken stones the wood splintered to straw
Which burst from the dismembered body—

The fragments torn out of the ruins
Are magic torn out of my mind
Are vision torn out of my eyes
Are spirit torn out of my soul—

And what the ruins leave which I can think
Into the city of my brain
Is forced abstractions and tired memories
A senseless lightless voiceless theatre
Where the ghosts play at being ghosts—

The old at wading waist-deep in the dust
The young at being lustreless—

My own existence dwelling in my body
Seems like an odour sicklied under rubble

A taste of marrow in the taste of bones
Tormented into apathy by shame—

The shame of what I never was
That when I lived my life among these dead
I did not live enough—

that when I loved
Among these dead—I did not love enough—
That when I looked the murderers in their eyes
I did not die enough—

                    I lacked
That which makes cities not to fall
The drop of agonizing sweat which changes
Into impenetrable crystal upon crosses
Which bear cathedrals—

                    the will
Which breathes its upward music into domes
Through flutes of springing columns—

                    the love
Which holds each moment to each moment
With architecture of continual passion.

Weep, Girl, Weep

Weep, girl, weep, for you have cause to weep.
His face is uprooted from your sleep,
His eyes torn from your eyes, dream from your dream.
Where you were by the window all one night
A million stars wore too faint a light
To show his machine
Plunge dark through dark out of sight.

    The wet tears on your face gleam
Down spires of the cathedral,
And in the crowded squares your lament
Makes a great angel whose instrument
Is strung on the heart behind the face of all.

The Angel

(TO W. G.)

Each is involved in the tears and blood of all.
Under the dreams of each move those unsleeping journeys—
The Will, the Lament, the Fall.

We have no inviolate instants where we are
Solid happiness hewn from day, set apart
From the others afar.

Human islands under their seas have roots
Spread through the multitude's fretful blood,
And to passionate childhoods.

To steel the will against awareness would banish
The angel who arrives each instant
From the horrific flesh;

Who warns that power, fear, agony, are the life under many;
That the real is the terrible; that to deny
This, unsheathes tyranny.

Listen, for his voice offers charity, hope, freedom—
Beggared charity, false hope, freedom to weep. True, and
    yet
He is truth's own doom
Blowing news of evil on a golden trumpet.

Epilogue to a Human Drama

When pavements were blown up, exposing nerves,
And the gas mains burned blue and gold
And stucco houses were smashed to a cloud
Pungent with mice, dust, garlic, anxiety:
When the reverberant emptied façades
Of the palaces of commerce,
Isolated in a vacuum of silence, suddenly
Cracked and roared and fell, and the seven-maned
Golden lions licked the stony fragments:

Then the only voice through deserted streets
Was the Cassandra bell which rang and rang and ran
As if released at last by time
Towards those fires that burst through many walls—
Prophetic doom opened to the nostrils,
Blood and fire streaming from the stones.

The City burned with unsentimental dignity
Of resigned wisdom: those stores and churches
Which had glittered emptily in gold and silk,
Stood near the crowning dome of the cathedral
Like courtiers round the Royal Martyr.
August shadows of night
And bursting days of concentrated light
Dropped from the skies to paint a final scene—
Illuminated agony of frowning stone.
Who can wonder then that every word
In burning London seemed out of a play?

On the stage, there were heroes, maidens, fools,
Victims, a chorus. The heroes were brave,
The rescued appeared passively beautiful,
The fools spat jokes into the skull of death,
The victims waited with the humble patience
Of animals trapped behind a wall
For the pickaxes to break with sun and water.
The chorus assisted, bringing cups of tea,
Praising the heroes, discussing the habits of the wicked,
Underlining the moral, explaining doom and truth.

Rejoice in the Abyss

(TO F. C. C.)

When the foundations quaked and the pillars shook
I trembled, and in the dark I feared
The photograph my skull might take
Through the eye sockets, in one flashlit instant
When the crumbling house would obliterate
Every impression of my sunlit life
In one image of final horror
Covering me with irrecoverable doom.

But the pulsation passed, and glass lay round me.
I rose from acrid dust, and in the night
I walked through clattering houses,
A prophet seeking tongues of flame.

Against a background of cloud, I saw
The houses kneel, exposed in their abject
Centennial selfish prayer: 'O Fate, this night
Save me from grief that punishes my neighbour!'
And the heads of all men living, cut open,
Would reveal the same shameless entreaty.

Then in the icy night, indifferent to our
Sulphurous nether fate, I saw
The dead of all time float on one calm tide
Among the foam of stars
Over the town, whose walls of brick and flesh
Are transitory dwellings
Of spirit journeying from birth to death.

The streets were filled with London prophets,
Saints of Covent Garden, Parliament Hill Fields,

Hampstead Heath, Lambeth and Saint Johns Wood
    Churchyard,
Who cried in cockney fanatic voices:
'In the midst of life is death!' And they all kneeled
And prayed against the misery manufactured
In mines and ships and mills, against
The greed of merchants, the vain hopes of churches,
And they played with children and marvelled at flowers,
And opened their low doors to invite in angels
Who had once climbed up sooty steeples
Like steeple jacks or chimney sweeps.

And they sang: 'We souls from the abyss,
Dancing in frozen peace of upper air,
Familiar with the fields of stars,
Say now: "Rejoice in the abyss!"
For hollow is the skull, the vacuum
Within the floating gold of Saint Paul's cross.
Unless your minds accept that emptiness
As the centre of your building and your love,
Under the bells of fox-gloves and of towers,
All human aims are stupefied denial
And each life feeds upon the grief of others
And the shamelessly entreating face
Of every man prays that he may be spared
Calamity that strikes each neighbouring face.'

A Man-made world

What a wild room
We enter, when the gloom
Of windowless night
Shuts us from the light

In a black, malicious box.
A freezing key locks
Us into utter dark
Where the nerves hark

For the man-made toys
To begin their noise.
The siren wails. After,
Broomsticks climb through air,

Then clocks burst through their springs,
Then the fire-bell rings.
Above and below comes
The anger of the drums.

Oh, what white rays gleaming
Against the sky's crouched ceiling!
What sudden flashes show
A woman who cries Oh!

In darkness where we are
With no saving star,
We hear the world we made
Pay back what we paid:

Money, steel, fire, stones,
Stripping flesh from bones,
With a wagging tongue of fear
Tormenting the ear,

Knocking at the outer skin,
To ask if any soul is in,
While the gloom descends
On our means become our ends.

The Conscript

On the turf's edge—grass flashing like a knife—
The conscript stands, above his native city.
He sees the sun's last rays consume that night
Whose tunnelled throat will swallow up the life
He's known—to thrust him on unknown tomorrow.
The sunset streaks the streets below with light.
He gazes on a red sky of self-pity
And sees his heart burn in a bowl of sorrow.

The action of tomorrow seems so real,
Necessity which will take him, so defined,
That this last night seems what he soon will feel,
Tomorrow's yesterday within his mind.
The setting sun belongs to a gold past
With the pathos of freedom left behind,
Discerned through blackening boughs of bitter contrast.

The hill grows pale, the strident colours fail,
An agate light encloses the home walls,
The gardens where his childhood played, are torn
Out of his eyes. Night's veil,
Dividing him from half his life, falls.

But then, beyond the rising star, appear
The armies marching to an earlier war.
The skeleton who strides last strikes the drum.
The conscript's soul is summoned to his eyes.
'Father!' he cries. 'Father! Father! I come!'

Almond Tree in a Bombed City

In the burned city, I see
The almond flower, as though
With great cathedral-fall
Barbarian rage set free
The angel of a fresco
From a cloister wall.

This flesh-petalled tree,
Angel of Fra Angelico,
With folded hands, bended knee
And arc of eloquent wing
(See the plumes like tongues grow
Promising the rainbow!),
To our world of ash will bring
Annunciation of Spring.

Responsibility: The Pilots who Destroyed Germany, Spring, 1945

I stood on a roof-top and they wove their cage,
Their murmuring, throbbing cage, in the air of blue crystal,
I saw them gleam above the town like diamond bolts
Conjoining invisible struts of wire,
Carrying through the sky their squadrons' cage
Woven by instincts delicate as a shoal of flashing fish.

They went. They left a silence in our streets below
Which boys gone to schoolroom leave in their play-ground:
A silence of asphalt, of privet hedge, of staring wall.
In the blue emptied sky their diamonds had scratched
Long curving finest whitest lines.
These the days soon melted into satin ribbons
Falling over heaven's terraces near the sun.

Oh, that April morning they carried my will
Exalted expanding singing in their aerial cage.
They carried my will. They dropped it on a German town.
My will exploded. Tall buildings fell down.

Then, when the ribbons faded, and the sky forgot,
And April was concerned with building nests and being hot
I began to remember the lost names and faces.

Now I tie the ribbons torn down from those terraces
Around the most hidden image in my lines,
And my life, which never paid the price of their wounds,
Turns thoughts over and over like a propeller,
Assumes their guilt, honours, repents, prays for them.

Tom's A-cold

Such a day such a day when the rain
Makes sky and plain one dull pain

When noon is mirror of mud
And tonight will be moon of blood,

Such a day was the sum of my life
On this plain in this house with my wife

In this world where my charcoal days
Burned with a hidden blaze.

I went clothed in herringbone tweed,
A grey shell, through which my bald head

Poked, like a nut, bare and lined.
My face was mask for my mind.

I sat through the days as at table,
Pre-posthumously respectable,

And after dessert I could see
Time's worms turn and feed on me.

The intelligence gleamed in my eyes
Bright chips of fallen skies,

Whose grey vagueness recalled that joke
Old-world schoolchildren would poke

At me, as a boy: 'Tom's a poet,
Although, Tom, Tom, he don't know it.'

Well, I used to ride on my bicycle
Down the country lanes, mile after mile,

And I'd think: 'How everything descends,
Clouds in the sky trailing dark horsetail ends,

'And at country fairs, the people with their hopes
Like puppets hung down from the sky on ropes

'By a time-machine which soon will jog them down
Two feet deep in mud of king and clown.'

Forgive my old ways, but you come too late
To find my rhyming up-to-date,

Where your stilted galosh on grey mud squirms
Over me, at my feast of worms.

Well, the others said: 'Life ascends, like a plant.'
But to me the sum of things seemed aslant,

Diagonal downward pressure of rain,
The waters driving under the plain.

Each dawn when I first opened eyelid
I seemed to lift a pyramid

Off appearances: this world seemed transparent
And, through its show, there were apparent

The folk reclining among roots
In villages under my boots.

Through a looking glass I watched my uncouth
Skeleton starve on the bare truth.

39

A tumulus outlined the strata
Where flint-arrows pointed to data

Of those planned cities underground
Where the hierarchic bones are wound

In robes of rock, vaguening in shape
Back to that aristocrat, the ape.

For junketings, I entrained to the city
Where fogs pencilled humanity

Packed in penthouses, as in ships
Waiting at quay-side, till each slips

Out on the tide, bearing its cargo
Of passions to the world below.

The Red Light districts and the modish sins
Reminded me of animal skins,

Skin of snake, fur of cat, pelt of bear,
With the sense of eyes which had once looked there.

And I loved old attics where the lumber
Of past centuries seemed to slumber:

Faded silk, muslin pokes, hip baths, warming pans,
Rhinoceros horn, flint locks, armour, sedans,

Imagine the ladies and gentlemen
Of whose rolling souls these were the skin,
Chairs, beds, hats, clothes, they were snug in.

Shells and hides which left a trail
As over my grave, in his shell, sir, that snail.

Well, well, musing thus, it seemed incumbent
I should sympathise with the recumbent,

Who rolled in mud and clay of facts
And from flesh and blood moulded their acts.

I noted the wish of prostitutes
To sleep prematurely among roots,

I observed the baby's or the great lady's mouth
Tormented with desire as with drouth,

And the dark passions of the city
Wresting pleasure from steel reality,

Such I understood. I was there with all
Who thrust against life like a wall,

And who, in action and in thought,
Upon their harsh condition wrought

Some passionate image, to prove
Their naked need could shape their love.

I understood the sick botched lives,
The drink, the whoring and the knives.

Well, what I abhorred were the great claims
Of inhuman superhuman aims

Attaching many to their gains
And making men links in their chains.

The wars, the abstract cause, false knowledge,
Exalting imperial privilege,

And in faith's name, the dubious creed
Usurping the single human need

Of knowing that we nothing know
Of whence we come and where we go

And nothing have, except we can
Comfort that poor condition, man.

They called me pessimist in my day
Yet perhaps I was happier than they,

Living in life as in the hollow
Earth which I now lie below.

Within life always, as in the bone,
Part of all life, and thus alone.

I was imprisoned in each feature
Like nature whistling within nature,

The individual universal
Spirit shut in the animal.

I dwelt within my hollow minute
Like the song within the flute,

And where the song breathed through the hole
You may call, if you like, my soul:

That prince shut in a lonely tower
Robbed of hereditary power.

Now where I lie in gravestone rhyme,
My eyes are these two pools which climb

Through grey reflections to the sky—
My world asking your world: 'Why?'

Word

The word bites like a fish.
Shall I throw it back free
Arrowing to that sea
Where thoughts lash tail and fin?
Or shall I pull it in
To rhyme upon a dish?

Empty House

Then, when the child was gone,
I was alone
In the house, suddenly grown huge. Each noise
Explained its cause away,
Animal, vegetable, mineral,
Nail, creaking board, or mouse.
But mostly there was quiet of after battle
Where round the room still lay
The soldiers and the paintbox, all the toys.
Then, when I went to tidy these away,
My hands refused to serve:
My body was the house,
And everything he'd touched, an exposed nerve.

Madonna

Below the scallop shell
Of the fanned sky
The clear girl is seated.
Her eyes are flowers
Thought by her body.
Her flesh a cloud
Edged with gold by her son.

The life in her life
Crouching to be born
Is head-downwards
In a lower room.
Inner flesh of peace
Withdrawn in a world
Where love makes the Real,
While the abstract Furies
Hunt the cities outside.

Her clear gaze divides
The world into two worlds:
Of kings who bring myrrh
To worship this birth:
Of heroes whose rays
Murder in the womb
Prenatal generations
Of reincarnate earth.
Her son will say: Choose!

Epithalamion

If my will could become this night
With all my conscious stars to witness
The marriage of this human pair—
Their fitness
The majesty upon my air—

And canopied beneath my trees
Their limbs on moss among my flowers—
My whisper of blessings and sighs
Would conspire with their own powers
Their furthest love to realize.

That they who in passionate meeting
Physically interpenetrate,
Should have my universe as bed
To lie down early there and late
By close and remote days re-wed.

That their explored happiness
Of mingled far discourse, should be
Stretched beyond this sheeted space
Where their curling limbs agree,
Into a timeless bodiless grace.

When them the hiding seas divide,
That their invisible presences
Should mingle between land and land:
All separating differences
Should be their hand reaching their hand.

Within this dragon-haunted era,
Let these two their faith perfect
To dome within their meeting mind
One clear sky of the intellect
Which no ill fate can make unkind.

O flesh and spirit of charity
Hammer that ring from their fused minute
Moulten where they are, part to part,
Whose circle appears absolute
And of the pure gold of the heart.

But I am not this night, I am
Only their well-wishing friend.
So, like this night, light by light,
I bring my presence to an end
With thoughts which are invisible
To make their loving possible.

O love, be indivisible!

Memento

Remember the blackness of that flesh
Tarring the bones with a thin varnish
Belsen Theresenstadt Buchenwald where
Faces were clenched fists of prayer
Knocking at the bird-song-fretted air.
Their eyes sunk jellied in their holes
Were held toward the sun like begging bowls
Their hands like rakes with fingernails of rust
Scratched for kindness from a little dust.
To many, in its beak no dove brought answer.

Speaking to the Dead
in the Language of the Dead

I

So this young man reeled out
Of gambling den or brothel—
                      his face white
His hair ebony—
              his waistcoat
Embroidered with small roses among stains
Of wine—

He drove into the night—
Hooves cannoned snow to moonlit smoke—
Black buttocks tossed under the sparkling bells—

Remote childhood towers mourned his life

Pursuit of happiness had exploded
A mine within his mind.

The lamentable word AGAIN
Exploded in his brain.

II

      He ran past stone dogs of the palace gate
Up arching stairways aching like his head
Into his room—
              flung himself down
His world revolving—
                  on his bed.

Then, through the darkness, images

Fixed into angels and devils of his pages.

'Again,' he sighed, 'Again.'

III

Within that darkness where I see his room
  —Floor of black flame, star-pointed ceiling—
Within this midnight and beyond his tomb,
  He incised with a quill his vein of feeling
And wound the thin red blood out through the gloom
  To set down here for us: revealing
The dancer, his despair, at which we look—
His blood behind the white mask of his book.

Passion of women, flushed from his embracing,
  He dipped his pen in: his great night-limbed lovers
In operative moments of enlacing
  Were experiments in sensuous manoeuvres
From which he formed those tears and blushes gracing
  Today's libraries: and that sigh, which hovers
Through spaces between letters, white and far,
Is on his page the print of what we are.

His moon, *his* nightingale, torn from his time,
  Her tear, falling down centuries, hour by hour,
Her letter, weeping her wish through his rhyme,
  Her footstep, immanent: from such, his tower
Whose base stands in depraved quicklime,
  But whose high gleam reintegrates the flower,
Petal by petal, of time-outworn fashion,
In omnipresent coexistent passion.

It was enough for him that what is, is,
  To cut his jewels on time like jewels in clocks.

The tears, the diamonds, duels, moons, the kisses,
   He shut within his stanzas' iron locks
For us to look at. What was, what lived, is his
   Ecstasy. Marriage, ennui, pox,
And passion's disenchantment were unreal.
   His life was the bright cutting edge we feel.

   Enough to praise it all. To burn! To live!
      Dip women, cards, remorse, and hell-rake fires,
   In the poetical preservative!
      Brush all the nightingales to wires
   Strung on the trees, behind a sigh! Oh give
      The ultimate affirmation when the choirs
   Mass onto silence. Beyond ultimate harm
   End with that opening 'O'! Death, like a charm!

IV
How is it
Your songs have sails which glide through death
And your transfigured head
Bends back futures to obeisant waves,
And your name like a deck as fresh as paint
Bridges that crowded hold
Loaded with ore of still-impassioned days
Fulgurant through our limbs? And you
Sail into our world yet still are you,
Blotches deleted from your brow
Where now the laurel scarcely dares
Bruise with praise the skin,
And future ages trembling here
Have thoughts like footprints across snow?

V
Perhaps we live in time as on a plain

Where our life is the blurred and jagged edge
Of all who ever died. We who are here
Fight out the fierce obsession of our wills
Upon each other's lives. Our violence
Enslaves our knowledge to our ignorance.

Yet in our feeling darkness, we are near
The sculptural presence of an influence
From the perfecting dead. Their night
Is words and statues and our light.
As though to live were to be doomfully blind
While the dead work within our living mind
Their art of chiaroscura,
Using our darkness that they may grow clear.

Here on our edge of clamant inexperience
We use for murder our creating powers,
And, building, destroy spiritual towers.
Yet under blood and mire upon our hands
The dead move through us into ordered lands.

You who once wandered through this maze of being
We suffer now we are, become all you
Quickening through the darkness of our seeing,
More than you lived. Through us the true
Is purged of pitiless irrelevance
Where on our harsh edge of existence
You gain your quiet and white significance.

Through us you enter into your ideal,
Through us the formless dream becomes the real,
Our life bears your death-purified statue
Within this restless world you also knew.

We Cannot Hold onto the World

We cannot hold onto the world
However much we would
We stand on a turning wheel and are hurled
Beyond evil and good.

That running boy with mouth raised up
As though to kiss the winning cup—
Chest, flying buttress of the tape—
Eyes like thrown stars: lies on the ground
His fires drawn out with no sound
Through the narrow bullet wound.

That woman like a Muse, whose gaze
Stared through her contemporaries
Lighting their thoughts on floors of seas:
Filled her dress with large stones
And lay beneath an icy brook
Her beautiful eyes broken
Her mind unstrung—a mirror of unspoken
Thoughts (white now as her bones)
Pages of an unwritten book.

A turning wheel scatters
Stars upon the wind.
Who shall regain
The concentrated mind
From blowing dust outside, and seas, and driving rain?

Time in our Time

Moving upwards through space, heaped with Now,
O self of each phenomenal instant,
Moving from inconceivable beginning
To inconceivable end—
                    Upon Time,
I was cast naked out of non-existence,
Upon this stair climbing between the stars,
Lifted some steps on Time,
Soon to reject me, thrown-down card,
Cadaver planing and spiralling through dark,
Dissolving into dust, dissolving into space.

Tomorrow and yesterday are pictures
Remembered and foreseen, painted within
Man's two profiles facing Past and Future, pivoted
On the irreducible secret diamond
His Now. Past and Future, pictures only,
And all events and places distant from
The instant of perception in the brain,
Are memories and prophecies.
All distant times and places, all events
In other minds, all knowledge folded
In books, Pasts petrified in statues,
Spatial distances witnessed by telescopes,
Prehuman histories embossed on fossils,
Silent messages from star to star,
Exist only in the flash within the single flesh.

Yet some Pasts do persist within the Now,
Within the Now some Futures lift
Witnessing trumpets blowing prophecies

Of stones which will bud into cities.
The snow-white Akropolis collects
Many eyes of dead Greeks from far histories
Held now in living eyes. It is
A column through Time, stone doves ascending
A prayer of skies, a ring of changes
Reintegrating each instant into Athens.

Oh save me in this day, when Now
Is a towering pillar of dust which sucks
The ruin of a world into its column.
When to perceive is to be part of that cloud
Whose castle changes into dragon.
Oh, though the Past dissolve, may all that was
Once idea integrated into stone
Enter my secret mind at the whirling centre
Of the external storm: and combine with
A love which penetrates through falling flesh
To paint the image in my heart
Of that past greatness and that once-willed Future,
Beyond the storm, which still can make a world.

Acknowledgments and Note

Nine Sketches for 'Returning to Vienna, 1947', were published in a limited edition by the Banyan Press, Paulet, Vermont, at the end of 1947. About three hundred copies of this edition were for sale.

Versions of several of these poems have appeared in *The New Statesman and Nation*, *The Listener*, *Horizon*, *Time and Tide*, *The New Yorker*, *Poetry*, *The Nation*, *Wake*, *Voices*, and in my book about Civil Defence, entitled *Citizens in War and After*.

A version of 'Speaking to the Dead in the Language of the Dead' was read by me at the Harvard Phi Beta Kappa Celebrations in June, 1948, and of 'Tom's A-Cold' at Columbia University Phi Beta Kappa Celebrations in the same month.

Acknowledgments are due to the editors of the publications mentioned above: and, if my memory be at fault, to any others to whom acknowledgment is due.

It should be noted that nearly all the poems which have appeared previously are now considerably altered. I wish to thank those friends who have given me advice and criticism; and particularly Frances Cornford.

S. S.